Mileage Log for Truck

Small Business Work Truck & Pickup Mileage Tracker for Tax Deductions - Clean, Easy, Tax-Ready Records

A. Herrick

Herrick, A.

Mileage Log for Truck: Small Business Work Truck & Pickup Mileage Tracker for Tax Deductions — Clean, Easy, Tax-Ready Records

First edition
Christiansted, US Virgin Islands: A. Herrick, 2026

VIII, 109 pages, 6 by 9 inches

Business | Accounting Records and Bookkeeping | Mileage|

ISBN 978-1-960427-67-0

LCCN – Not assigned

657.2

the publisher and the author have made every effort to ensure that the information in this book was correct at press time, and while this publication is designed to provide accurate information in regard to the subject matter covered, the publisher and the author assume no responsibility for errors, inaccuracies, omissions, or any other inconsistencies herein and hereby disclaim any liability to any party for any loss, damage, or disruption caused by errors or omissions, whether such errors or omissions result from negligence, accident, or any other cause. If any names are used in any illustration, they have been changed to protect the privacy of the individual.

Mileage Log for Truck

Not for OTR/CDL/IFTA use.

Vehicle Make / Model / Year _____________________

VIN (Vehicle Identification Number)

____ (OPTIONAL)

License Plate Number _____________________ (OPTIONAL)

Business Name _________________________________

Owner Name ___________________________________

Contact Number / Email _________________________

Purchase Date _________________________________

Date placed in service __________________________

Purchase Price ________________________________

Beginning Odometer _______________________Date_________

Ending Odometer _________________________Date_________

Primary Business Use (check all that apply):
☐ Jobsite travel ☐ Service calls ☐ Supplies pickup
☐ Client visits ☐ Deliveries ☐ Equipment hauling
☐ Other: _______________________________

Vehicle Change Page for Truck

What if you change Vehicles mid-year? You will need this page to record it:

Selling price of the prior vehicle $________________________

Date of sale____

Vehicle Make / Model / Year ______________________________

VIN (Vehicle Identification Number)

____ (OPTIONAL)

License Plate Number ____________________ (OPTIONAL)

Business Name ____

Owner Name ____

Contact Number / Email _________________________________

Purchase Date ____

Date placed in service __________________________________

Purchase Price ____

Beginning Odometer ____________________Date________

Ending Odometer ______________________Date________

Primary Business Use (check all that apply):
☐ Jobsite travel ☐ Service calls ☐ Supplies pickup
☐ Client visits ☐ Deliveries ☐ Equipment hauling
☐ Other: _______________________________

Content

Quick Start   2

Disclaimer   3

Purpose Phrases for Pickup & Work Truck   4

Standard Mileage Rates   5

Load/Haul Notes (Optional)   6

Fuel Tracker Pages (Optional)   8

Service & Maintenance Log Pages (Optional)   12

Mixed-Use Reality Check & Log Pages   16

Mileage Log for Truck   56

Monthly Summary Pages (Recommended)   94

Tax-Time Checklist   107

Year-End Preparation Checklist   108

Annual Summary   109

Quick Start

This edition is built for pickup and work-truck owners who use their vehicle for business, service calls, jobsite visits, supply runs, and daily operations.

Keep it simple: record the trip + purpose + mileage.

Capacity: space for **1,000+ trip entries.**

This logbook is designed to help you maintain IRS-style records for business mileage. For each trip, record the date, starting and ending odometer readings, total miles driven, and the business purpose.

Add parking and tolls when applicable.

Complete each entry on the day the trip occurs.

At the end of every month, use the Monthly Summary pages to confirm totals and verify your odometer readings.

Keeping accurate, timely records ensures you have everything you need for year-end reporting or tax preparation.

Disclaimer

This logbook is a recordkeeping tool. It is **not** legal or tax advice. If you're unsure how to classify trips for your situation, consult a qualified tax professional

Purpose Phrases for Pickup & Work Trucks

- Jobsite visit

- Client visit

- Service call

- Supply run

- Materials pickup

- Equipment pickup/return

- Delivery / drop-off

- Banking / deposits

- Shipping / mailing

- Business meeting

- Training / certification

- Vendor visit

Tip: If you haul or carry equipment, a short note like "equipment delivery" makes the record feel real.

Tax year: ______________________

Standard mileage rate (check IRS):

Business ______ per mile

Medical ______ per mile

Charity ______ per mile

Load / Haul Notes (Optional)

This is **not** a CDL/IFTA log. These pages exist for real-life context.

Date Trip Purpose   What Was Hauled (brief) Notes

____

____

____

____

____

____

____

____

____

____

____

____

____

Fuel Tracker Pages
(Optional)

Date Amount   Location   Odometer   Gallons

____

____

____

____

____

____

____

____

____

____

____

____

____

____

Fuel Tracker Pages
(Optional)

Date Amount   Location   Odometer   Gallons

Fuel Tracker Pages
(Optional)

Date Amount   Location   Odometer   Gallons

Fuel Tracker Pages
(Optional)

Date Amount   Location   Odometer   Gallons

Fuel Tracker Pages
(Optional)

Date Amount   Location   Odometer   Gallons

Service & Maintenance Log Pages
(Optional)

Date   Amount   Vendor Service Notes Odometer Warranty Period

Service & Maintenance Log Pages
(Optional)

Date   Amount   Vendor   Service   Notes   Odometer   Warranty Period

Service & Maintenance Log Pages
(Optional)

Date   Amount   Vendor Service   Notes   Odometer   Warranty Period

Mixed-Use Reality Check & Log Pages

Most pickup owners use their truck for everything. That's fine — just don't turn your mileage log into a guessing game.

What helps your records:

- Write the purpose every time

- Keep the mileage consistent

- Add notes on mixed-stop days

- Don't "estimate later" (later becomes never)

Multiple Stops Day Log (Stops: ___) Date: _______

Start Odometer: ________ End Odometer: ________

Total Business Miles: __________________________

Stops / Notes:

____

____

____

____

____

____

____

____

____

____

____

Multiple Stops Day Log (Stops: ___) Date: _______

Start Odometer: ________ End Odometer: ________

Total Business Miles: __________________________

Stops / Notes:

____

____

____

____

____

____

____

____

____

____

Multiple Stops Day Log (Stops: ___) Date: ______

Start Odometer: _________ End Odometer: _________

Total Business Miles: __________________________

Stops / Notes:

____

____

____

____

____

____

____

____

____

____

Multiple Stops Day Log (Stops: ___) Date: _______

Start Odometer: ________ End Odometer: ________

Total Business Miles: __________________________

Stops / Notes:

Multiple Stops Day Log (Stops: ___) Date: _______

Start Odometer: _________ End Odometer: _________

Total Business Miles: _____________________________

Stops / Notes:

____

____

____

____

____

____

____

____

____

____

Multiple Stops Day Log (Stops: ___) Date: _______

Start Odometer: _________ End Odometer: _________

Total Business Miles: ____________________________

Stops / Notes:

____

____

____

____

____

____

____

____

____

____

Multiple Stops Day Log (Stops: ___) Date: _______

Start Odometer: ________ End Odometer: ________

Total Business Miles: ______________________________

Stops / Notes:

____

____

____

____

____

____

____

____

____

____

____

Multiple Stops Day Log (Stops: ___) Date: ______

Start Odometer: ________   End Odometer: ________

Total Business Miles: __________________________

Stops / Notes:

____

____

____

____

____

____

____

____

____

____

Multiple Stops Day Log (Stops: ___) Date: _______

Start Odometer: _________   End Odometer: _________

Total Business Miles: ______________________________

Stops / Notes:

____

____

____

____

____

____

____

____

____

____

Multiple Stops Day Log (Stops: ___) Date: _______

Start Odometer: _________   End Odometer: _________

Total Business Miles: ______________________________

Stops / Notes:

____

____

____

____

____

____

____

____

____

____

Multiple Stops Day Log (Stops: ___) Date: _______

Start Odometer: _________ End Odometer: _________

Total Business Miles: ____________________________

Stops / Notes:

____

____

____

____

____

____

____

____

____

____

Multiple Stops Day Log (Stops: ___) Date: _______

Start Odometer: _________ End Odometer: _________

Total Business Miles: _______________________________

Stops / Notes:

____

____

____

____

____

____

____

____

____

____

Multiple Stops Day Log (Stops: ___) Date: ______

Start Odometer: _________   End Odometer: _________

Total Business Miles: ___________________________

Stops / Notes:

Multiple Stops Day Log (Stops: ___) Date: _______

Start Odometer: _________ End Odometer: _________

Total Business Miles: ___________________________

Stops / Notes:

Multiple Stops Day Log (Stops: ___) Date: _______

Start Odometer: _________ End Odometer: _________

Total Business Miles: ___________________________

Stops / Notes:

Multiple Stops Day Log (Stops: ___) Date: _______

Start Odometer: ________ End Odometer: ________

Total Business Miles: __________________________

Stops / Notes:

____

____

____

____

____

____

____

____

____

____

Multiple Stops Day Log (Stops: ___) Date: _______

Start Odometer: _________ End Odometer: _________

Total Business Miles: __________________________

Stops / Notes:

____

____

____

____

____

____

____

____

____

____

Multiple Stops Day Log (Stops: ___) Date: _______

Start Odometer: __________   End Odometer: __________

Total Business Miles: ________________________________

Stops / Notes:

____

____

____

____

____

____

____

____

____

____

Multiple Stops Day Log (Stops: ____) Date: _________

Start Odometer: __________ End Odometer: __________

Total Business Miles: ______________________________

Stops / Notes:

____

____

____

____

____

____

____

____

____

____

Multiple Stops Day Log (Stops: ___) Date: ______

Start Odometer: _________   End Odometer: _________

Total Business Miles: _________________________

Stops / Notes:

____

____

____

____

____

____

____

____

____

____

Multiple Stops Day Log (Stops: ___) Date: ______

Start Odometer: _________ End Odometer: _________

Total Business Miles: ______________________________

Stops / Notes:

____

____

____

____

____

____

____

____

____

____

____

Multiple Stops Day Log (Stops: ___) Date: ______

Start Odometer: _________   End Odometer: _________

Total Business Miles: __________________________

Stops / Notes:

Multiple Stops Day Log (Stops: ___) Date: ______

Start Odometer: _________ End Odometer: _________

Total Business Miles: _______________________________

Stops / Notes:

____

____

____

____

____

____

____

____

____

____

Multiple Stops Day Log (Stops: ____) Date: ________

Start Odometer: __________ End Odometer: __________

Total Business Miles: ________________________________

Stops / Notes:

____

____

____

____

____

____

____

____

____

____

Multiple Stops Day Log (Stops: ___) Date: _______

Start Odometer: _________ End Odometer: _________

Total Business Miles: _______________________________

Stops / Notes:

____

____

____

____

____

____

____

____

____

____

____

Multiple Stops Day Log (Stops: ___) Date: ______

Start Odometer: _________ End Odometer: _________

Total Business Miles: __________________________

Stops / Notes:

Multiple Stops Day Log (Stops: ___) Date: ______

Start Odometer: _________   End Odometer: _________

Total Business Miles: _________________________

Stops / Notes:

____

____

____

____

____

____

____

____

____

____

Multiple Stops Day Log (Stops: ___) Date: _______

Start Odometer: _________ End Odometer: _________

Total Business Miles: ___________________________

Stops / Notes:

____

____

____

____

____

____

____

____

____

____

____

Multiple Stops Day Log (Stops: ___) Date: ______

Start Odometer: _________ End Odometer: _________

Total Business Miles: _____________________________

Stops / Notes:

____

____

____

____

____

____

____

____

____

____

Multiple Stops Day Log (Stops: ___) Date: _______

Start Odometer: _________ End Odometer: _________

Total Business Miles: ___________________________

Stops / Notes:

____

____

____

____

____

____

____

____

____

____

Multiple Stops Day Log (Stops: ___) Date: ______

Start Odometer: ________ End Odometer: ________

Total Business Miles: ___________________________

Stops / Notes:

Multiple Stops Day Log (Stops: ___) Date: ______

Start Odometer: _________ End Odometer: _________

Total Business Miles: ______________________________

Stops / Notes:

____

____

____

____

____

____

____

____

____

____

____

Multiple Stops Day Log (Stops: ___) Date: _______

Start Odometer: _________ End Odometer: _________

Total Business Miles: _______________________________

Stops / Notes:

Multiple Stops Day Log (Stops: ___) Date: ______

Start Odometer: _________ End Odometer: _________

Total Business Miles: ___________________________

Stops / Notes:

Multiple Stops Day Log (Stops: ___) Date: _______

Start Odometer: _________ End Odometer: _________

Total Business Miles: _______________________________

Stops / Notes:

____

____

____

____

____

____

____

____

____

____

Multiple Stops Day Log (Stops: ___) Date: ______

Start Odometer: _________ End Odometer: _________

Total Business Miles: _________________________

Stops / Notes:

Multiple Stops Day Log (Stops: ___) Date: _______

Start Odometer: ________ End Odometer: ________

Total Business Miles: _________________________

Stops / Notes:

Multiple Stops Day Log (Stops: ___) Date: _______

Start Odometer: ________ End Odometer: ________

Total Business Miles: ___________________________

Stops / Notes:

____

____

____

____

____

____

____

____

____

____

Multiple Stops Day Log (Stops: ___) Date: _______

Start Odometer: _________   End Odometer: ________

Total Business Miles: ___________________________

Stops / Notes:

Mileage Log for Truck

Date	Starting Odometer	Ending Odometer	Total Miles	Purpose of Trip	Parking and Tolls Cost

Total

Mileage Log for Truck

Date	Starting Odometer	Ending Odometer	Total Miles	Purpose of Trip	Parking and Tolls Cost
			57		

Total

Mileage Log for Truck

Date	Starting Odometer	Ending Odometer	Total Miles	Purpose of Trip	Parking and Tolls Cost

Total

Mileage Log for Truck

Date	Starting Odometer	Ending Odometer	Total Miles	Purpose of Trip	Parking and Tolls Cost

Total

Mileage Log for Truck

Date	Starting Odometer	Ending Odometer	Total Miles	Purpose of Trip	Parking and Tolls Cost

Total

Mileage Log for Truck

Date	Starting Odometer	Ending Odometer	Total Miles	Purpose of Trip	Parking and Tolls Cost

Total

Mileage Log for Truck

Date	Starting Odometer	Ending Odometer	Total Miles	Purpose of Trip	Parking and Tolls Cost

Total

Mileage Log for Truck

Date	Starting Odometer	Ending Odometer	Total Miles	Purpose of Trip	Parking and Tolls Cost

Total

Mileage Log for Truck

Date	Starting Odometer	Ending Odometer	Total Miles	Purpose of Trip	Parking and Tolls Cost

Total

Mileage Log for Truck

Date	Starting Odometer	Ending Odometer	Total Miles	Purpose of Trip	Parking and Tolls Cost

Total

Mileage Log for Truck

Date	Starting Odometer	Ending Odometer	Total Miles	Purpose of Trip	Parking and Tolls Cost

Total

Mileage Log for Truck

Date	Starting Odometer	Ending Odometer	Total Miles	Purpose of Trip	Parking and Tolls Cost

Total

Mileage Log for Truck

Date	Starting Odometer	Ending Odometer	Total Miles	Purpose of Trip	Parking and Tolls Cost

Total

Mileage Log for Truck

Date	Starting Odometer	Ending Odometer	Total Miles	Purpose of Trip	Parking and Tolls Cost

Total

Mileage Log for Truck

Date	Starting Odometer	Ending Odometer	Total Miles	Purpose of Trip	Parking and Tolls Cost

Total

Mileage Log for Truck

Date	Starting Odometer	Ending Odometer	Total Miles	Purpose of Trip	Parking and Tolls Cost

Total

Mileage Log for Truck

Date	Starting Odometer	Ending Odometer	Total Miles	Purpose of Trip	Parking and Tolls Cost

Total

Mileage Log for Truck

Date	Starting Odometer	Ending Odometer	Total Miles	Purpose of Trip	Parking and Tolls Cost

Total

Mileage Log for Truck

Date	Starting Odometer	Ending Odometer	Total Miles	Purpose of Trip	Parking and Tolls Cost
			74		

Total

Mileage Log for Truck

Date	Starting Odometer	Ending Odometer	Total Miles	Purpose of Trip	Parking and Tolls Cost

Total

Mileage Log for Truck

Date	Starting Odometer	Ending Odometer	Total Miles	Purpose of Trip	Parking and Tolls Cost

Total

Mileage Log for Truck

Date	Starting Odometer	Ending Odometer	Total Miles	Purpose of Trip	Parking and Tolls Cost

Total

Mileage Log for Truck

Date	Starting Odometer	Ending Odometer	Total Miles	Purpose of Trip	Parking and Tolls Cost
			78		

Total

Mileage Log for Truck

Date	Starting Odometer	Ending Odometer	Total Miles	Purpose of Trip	Parking and Tolls Cost

Total

Mileage Log for Truck

Date	Starting Odometer	Ending Odometer	Total Miles	Purpose of Trip	Parking and Tolls Cost

Total

Mileage Log for Truck

Date	Starting Odometer	Ending Odometer	Total Miles	Purpose of Trip	Parking and Tolls Cost

Total

Mileage Log for Truck

Date	Starting Odometer	Ending Odometer	Total Miles	Purpose of Trip	Parking and Tolls Cost

Total

Mileage Log for Truck

Date	Starting Odometer	Ending Odometer	Total Miles	Purpose of Trip	Parking and Tolls Cost

Total

Mileage Log for Truck

Date	Starting Odometer	Ending Odometer	Total Miles	Purpose of Trip	Parking and Tolls Cost

Total

Mileage Log for Truck

Date	Starting Odometer	Ending Odometer	Total Miles	Purpose of Trip	Parking and Tolls Cost

Total

Mileage Log for Truck

Date	Starting Odometer	Ending Odometer	Total Miles	Purpose of Trip	Parking and Tolls Cost

Total

Mileage Log for Truck

Date	Starting Odometer	Ending Odometer	Total Miles	Purpose of Trip	Parking and Tolls Cost

Total

Mileage Log for Truck

Date	Starting Odometer	Ending Odometer	Total Miles	Purpose of Trip	Parking and Tolls Cost

Total

Mileage Log for Truck

Date	Starting Odometer	Ending Odometer	Total Miles	Purpose of Trip	Parking and Tolls Cost

Total

Mileage Log for Truck

Date	Starting Odometer	Ending Odometer	Total Miles	Purpose of Trip	Parking and Tolls Cost

Total

Mileage Log for Truck

Date	Starting Odometer	Ending Odometer	Total Miles	Purpose of Trip	Parking and Tolls Cost

Total

Mileage Log for Truck

Date	Starting Odometer	Ending Odometer	Total Miles	Purpose of Trip	Parking and Tolls Cost

Total

Mileage Log for Truck

Date	Starting Odometer	Ending Odometer	Total Miles	Purpose of Trip	Parking and Tolls Cost

Total

Monthly Summary Pages
(Recommended)

January Monthly Summary

Monthly Mileage Audit-Ready Checklist

☐ All trip purposes clearly labeled

☐ Monthly totals completed

☐ Odometer start and end recorded

Odometer Start ___________________________________

Odometer End ___________________________________

Total Miles ___________________________________

Total Miles – Business Miles = Personal Miles___________

Business Miles ___________________________________

Parking/Tolls $___________________________________

February Monthly Summary

Monthly Mileage Audit-Ready Checklist

☐ All trip purposes clearly labeled

☐ Monthly totals completed

☐ Odometer start and end recorded

Odometer Start ______________________________

Odometer End ______________________________

Total Miles ______________________________

Total Miles – Business Miles = Personal Miles____________

Business Miles ______________________________

Parking/Tolls $______________________________

March Monthly Summary

Monthly Mileage Audit-Ready Checklist

☐ All trip purposes clearly labeled

☐ Monthly totals completed

☐ Odometer start and end recorded

Odometer Start _______________________________

Odometer End _______________________________

Total Miles _______________________________

Total Miles – Business Miles = Personal Miles_____________

Business Miles _______________________________

Parking/Tolls $_______________________________

April Monthly Summary

Monthly Mileage Audit-Ready Checklist

☐ All trip purposes clearly labeled

☐ Monthly totals completed

☐ Odometer start and end recorded

Odometer Start ______________________________________

Odometer End ______________________________________

Total Miles ______________________________________

Total Miles – Business Miles = Personal Miles____________

Business Miles ______________________________________

Parking/Tolls $______________________________________

May Monthly Summary

Monthly Mileage Audit-Ready Checklist

☐ All trip purposes clearly labeled

☐ Monthly totals completed

☐ Odometer start and end recorded

Odometer Start ___________________________________

Odometer End ___________________________________

Total Miles ___________________________________

Total Miles – Business Miles = Personal Miles___________

Business Miles ___________________________________

Parking/Tolls $___________________________________

June Monthly Summary

Monthly Mileage Audit-Ready Checklist

☐ All trip purposes clearly labeled

☐ Monthly totals completed

☐ Odometer start and end recorded

Odometer Start   ____________________________

Odometer End   ____________________________

Total Miles   ____________________________

Total Miles – Business Miles = Personal Miles__________

Business Miles   ____________________________

Parking/Tolls $____________________________

July Monthly Summary

Monthly Mileage Audit-Ready Checklist

☐ All trip purposes clearly labeled

☐ Monthly totals completed

☐ Odometer start and end recorded

Odometer Start _______________________________

Odometer End _______________________________

Total Miles _______________________________

Total Miles – Business Miles = Personal Miles___________

Business Miles _______________________________

Parking/Tolls $_______________________________

August Monthly Summary

Monthly Mileage Audit-Ready Checklist

☐ All trip purposes clearly labeled

☐ Monthly totals completed

☐ Odometer start and end recorded

Odometer Start _______________________________________

Odometer End _______________________________________

Total Miles _______________________________________

Total Miles – Business Miles = Personal Miles___________

Business Miles _______________________________________

Parking/Tolls $_______________________________________

September Monthly Summary

Monthly Mileage Audit-Ready Checklist

☐ All trip purposes clearly labeled

☐ Monthly totals completed

☐ Odometer start and end recorded

Odometer Start _______________________________________

Odometer End _______________________________________

Total Miles _______________________________________

Total Miles – Business Miles = Personal Miles____________

Business Miles _______________________________________

Parking/Tolls $_________________________________

October Monthly Summary

Monthly Mileage Audit-Ready Checklist

☐ All trip purposes clearly labeled

☐ Monthly totals completed

☐ Odometer start and end recorded

Odometer Start   _______________________________________

Odometer End   _______________________________________

Total Miles   _______________________________________

Total Miles – Business Miles = Personal Miles___________

Business Miles   _______________________________________

Parking/Tolls $_______________________________________

November Monthly Summary

Monthly Mileage Audit-Ready Checklist

☐ All trip purposes clearly labeled

☐ Monthly totals completed

☐ Odometer start and end recorded

Odometer Start ______________________________________

Odometer End ______________________________________

Total Miles ______________________________________

Total Miles – Business Miles = Personal Miles____________

Business Miles ______________________________________

Parking/Tolls $______________________________________

December Monthly Summary

Monthly Mileage Audit-Ready Checklist

☐ All trip purposes clearly labeled

☐ Monthly totals completed

☐ Odometer start and end recorded

Odometer Start ____________________________________

Odometer End ____________________________________

Total Miles ____________________________________

Total Miles – Business Miles = Personal Miles____________

Business Miles ____________________________________

Parking/Tolls $__________________________________

Tax-Time Checklist

☐ Trips have purpose (jobsite, service call, supply run, etc.)

☐ Odometer start/end is recorded (or miles are clear)

☐ Monthly totals are completed (optional but helpful)

☐ If more than one vehicle is used, logs are clearly separated

☐ Notes exist for long days and multiple stops

Year-End Preparation Checklist

☐ All logs total per month

☐ Beginning and ending Odometer readings confirmed

☐ Data shared with your preparer

<u>NOTE FROM THE AUTHOR:</u>

Thank you for reading and using this mileage log designed especially for trucks.

If you found value in this book, please take a minute to leave a review.

Annual Summary

Odometer Start _______________________

Odometer End _______________________

Total Miles _______________________

Business Miles _______________________

Parking/Tolls $_______________________

Fuel $_______________________